CONTENTS

SONNET 100

SONNET 100

MARILYN ALLEN

TE
Textshop Editions

Clinton, MA ૪ Redondo Beach, CA
2021

Textshop Editions is a collaborative project
dedicated to producing limited series
of experimental writing.
It was founded by
K. A. Wisniewski & Piotr Florczyk.
More information may be found at
http://TextshopExperiments.org/TextshopEditions

Cataloging-in-Publication Data is available
at the Library of Congress

Library of Congress Control Number:
2021936401

First printing, April 2021

Book Design by K. A. Wisniewski

ISBN-13: 9781736465813

Printed in the United States of America

SONNET 100

PREFACE

Sonnet 100 is a collaboration between a human subject and a digital voice recognition system generated over the duration of 100 days. This collaborative text was produced in isolation during the COVID 19 pandemic when social media platforms and digital communication systems were exponentially embedded in the paradigm of human utterance. The dynamic between the human and the digital inevitably intensified during the social distancing measures imposed upon communities during the Coronavirus outbreak; a dynamic which arguably amplified the complexities of how meaning is distributed between human and digital voices. The premise of *Sonnet 100* is the potential for new narrative flows to be produced through anomalies generated between human speech and computational voice recognition.

Within *Sonnet 100* the condition of isolation induced by COVID 19 and the constraints imposed upon literary practices by the OuLiPo group are considered in parallel. Constraints are proposed as potential methods to generate a form of procedural poetics. OuLiPo is an acronym for Ouvroir de Littérature Potentielle, meaning Workshop for Potential Literature. The OuLiPo group rejected romantic notions of inspiration and spontaneity as sources of literary production and alternatively developed the concept of systematic writing. The OuLiPo group were "concerned not with literary works but with the structures and procedures capable of producing them."[1] On March 23, 2020, I, the human subject, spoke the words of Shakespeare's 100th sonnet into a computational voice recognition system where a new text was generated. This new text was then spoken into the same software to produce another new text; this process was repeated for 100 days, one iteration per day. *Sonnet 100* concluded on June 30, 2020.

The *Sonnet 100* human/digital collaboration generated one hundred new sonnets, one hundred possibilities amid a multiplicity of future texts which remain in a state of potentiality. Warren Motte, author of *Oulipo: A Primer of Potential Literature*, suggests; "a potential work is a work which is not limited to its appearances."[2] Giorgio Agamben's writing on potentiality also suggests that the text actualised or unfolded is only one possibility among other potential iterations. Agamben's collapse of the actual/potential dichotomy proposes that potentiality persists within that which is actualised, thus affording potentiality the same significance as actuality. "The multiplicity of the possible is here, it is now. It is intermediary between the phenomena [human/digital, actual/potential], it rustles in the midst of the forms that emerge from it."[3] Within *Sonnet 100* this space of potentiality is characterized through a principle of variance; the anomalous material generated through the human/digital relation. The human "machine produces a flow, another machine [voice recognition] coupled to this interrupts the flow."[4]

Sonnet 100 examines the intersection between the human machine and the digital machine, affirming this relation as a generative space for creative production. Our perception of creative production has traditionally adopted an asymmetric configuration wherein human authorship occupies a dominant position and our computational counterparts are consigned to perform a subsidiary role. Creativity is commonly considered to be the vestige of human cognition; however, with the proliferation of artificial intelligence systems and their capacity to compose and design, this assumption is less certain. A new paradigm may be said to exist whereby humans are relinquishing their role as 'author' and engaging in creative dialogues with technology. This social and cultural transition transforms both the perception and practice of creativity, engendering a new system for cultural production.

The linguistic transgressions generated between the human and digital subjects in *Sonnet 100* suggest a connection to Gilles Deleuze and Félix Guattari's writing on minor literatures. A minority is, in its common usage, perceived as subsidiary; a supplement or adjunct to a major ideology; however, a minor literature from a Deleuzoguattarian perspective is considered to operate from within the major language.

> [A] minor literature does not occur 'elsewhere' or 'apart from' a major literature (this is not a dialectic) but on the contrary operates from within, using the same elements as it were, but in a different manner.[5]

If a minor literature operates from within a major system, then a minoritarian holds the potential to generate disruption within a dominant ideology. Within *Sonnet 100*, the human voice occupies a majoritarian position (the major language) with accepted linguistic and semantic practices. The computational voice recognition software is positioned as minoritarian (a minor literature), operating from within the major language: A minor literature is both part of the major language and foreign to it. Deleuze suggests that a minor literature "opens up a kind of foreign language within language, which is neither another language nor a rediscovered patois, but a becoming-other of language, a minorisation of this major language, a delirium that carries it off [and] escapes the dominant system."[6] If a minor literature operates from within a major language then minor variations are implicit in major systems, variations understood as glitches, digressions, or a clinamen.

When the iteration of words and coherence of sentences within *Sonnet 100*'s one hundred repetitions are not entirely plausible, we begin to observe a rupture in the digital simulation of human voicing. Within these computational ruptures we perceive the interplay between sense and nonsense, difference and différance.

The textual glitches, ruptures and anomalies in *Sonnet 100* suggest deterritorialising gestures, which disrupt the strictures of contrivance and presupposition. The discourse between the human and digital subjects operates in a cultural space where malfunctioning, errancy and system failures are perceived as generative phenomena; aesthetic failures that create a cut in the flow of majoritarian striations. *Sonnet 100* is not an attempt to enact a process of translation from one system (human) to another (digital), but an elucidation of the textual secretions produced via digital stuttering. Deleuze describes stuttering as being distinct from speech, a zone of vibration where language itself is stretched.[7] When this stretching of language is recontextualized within the field of parapoetics it resists the derogatory classification of failure (the computational failure to accurately comprehend human speech) and adopts a generative position (the computational potential to create new textual gestures). Parapoetics is understood not as the poet's facility for invention or an intentional digression from tradition but as the aleatoric gesture of language and its relations.

Sonnet 100's exploration of writing via a human/digital machine explicates the effect of nuanced speech on digital perception. Over the period of 100 days the context within which text was spoken fluctuated; from changes in vocal intonation, breath and tempo, to background noise. This fluctuation is the "marking of the same territory [...] against the background of a variation in intensities between one parade and another."[8] Each textual parade of Shakespeare's poem was performed against a variation in intensities: A barking dog, a text alert, street noise, the physical effects of atmospheric conditions on vocal clarity, software glitches, battery failures and depleted bandwidth, all of which impacted upon the text generated by the computer's voice recognition system. This is a system wherein Shakespeare's plea "Where art thou, Muse" transgressed to "Where art thou, views" and "Whereabouts are you" and "When amounts you" and "One-man you" and "When money do" and so on. Shakespeare's call to the romanticist's muse is answered by a digital deconstruction of human authorship. Variations in the act of speaking and the subsequent semantic lapses generated by the computer's algorithmic attempts to identify spoken language establish a socio-technical form of literature where embodied speech and digital perception enter into a co-operative paradigm. *Sonnet 100* reconsiders the role of human authorship in a post-digital context through a metamodernist speculation on the dynamic reciprocity implicit in human/digital interaction.

Semantic blanks and irregular grammatical and syntactical formations resonate on the pages of *Sonnet 100*, doubtless leaving the conventional reader of poetry grasping for familiarity; however, *Sonnet 100* does not proffer coherent sentences and logical narratives, but rather demands the attention of the nonsensologist. The linguistic slips and digressions in this textual performance suggest a digital absurdism reminiscent of Edward Lear, Lewis Carroll and James Joyce. The principles of the literary absurd may provide a method with which to negotiate *Sonnet 100* and the data produced through our interactions with the digital; materials of both sense and nonsense.

bababadalgharaghtakamminarronnkonnbronntonnerronntuon-nthunntrovarrhounawnskawntoohoohoordenenthurnuk![9]

Speech recognition systems enable the speech-to-text process to be enacted and within this pseudo-conversational procedure an entropic dialogue between language and code is generated. A slight pause is perceptible between speech and its textual manifestation on the page, a hesitative, cognitive buffering. This process is reminiscent of our interactions with Siri where a technological pause between speech and response establishes a socio-technical rhythm. Speech recognition technologies are routinely confounded by regional accents and phonetic similarities resulting in a tacit acceptance of misunderstanding and linguistic mutation.

The interplay between the human and digital protagonists in *Sonnet 100* produces a feedback loop and "although speech and writing issuing from programmed media may still be recognizable as spoken utterances and print documents, they do not emerge unchanged by the encounter with code."[10] Interactions between human and digital subjects are commonly perceived as sterile encounters; however, the *Sonnet 100* speech-to-text machine engendered a process of reciprocity wherein the translation of "In gentle numbers time so idly spent" to 'Gentleman of concern' evoked a sensorial response; laughter!

Within *Sonnet 100* a multitude of divergent, often preposterous, linguistic constructions are generated from a single Shakespearean sonnet. "When the first sonnet was written almost a thousand years ago, what counted was not the poem itself but a new potentiality of future poems."[11]

REFERENCES

[1] Harry Mathews and Alistair Brotchie, ed., *Oulipo Compendium*, 2nd edition (London: Atlas Press, 2005), 213.

[2] Warren F. Motte, *Oulipo: A Primer of Potential Literature*, (Normal, IL: Dalkey Archive Press, 1998), 65.

[3] Michel Serres, *Genesis*, trans. Genevieve James & James Nielson (Ann Arbor, MI: University of Michigan Press, 1997), 23-24.

[4] Simon O'Sullivan, *Art Encounters Deleuze and Guattari: Thought Beyond Representation* (Hampshire UK: Palgrave Macmillan, 2006), 24.

[5] Simon O'Sullivan, "Notes Towards a Minor Art Practice," *Drain: Journal of Contemporary Art and Culture* 5 (October 2005), accessed May 17, 2013, http://www.drainmag.com/ contentNOVEMBER/RELATED_ESSAYS/Notes_Towards_ Minor_Practice.htm.

[6] Gilles Deleuze, *Essays Critical and Clinical*, trans. Daniel W. Smith & Michael A. Greco, (Minneapolis, MN: University of Minnesota Press, 1997), 5.

[7] Ibid, 108-109.

[8] James Williams, *Gilles Deleuze's Difference and Repetition: A Critical Introduction and Guide* (Edinburgh: Edinburgh University Press, 2003), 12.

[9] James Joyce, *Finnegans Wake*, (Ware, Hertfordshire Wordsworth Editions, 2012), 3.

[10] N. Katherine Hayles, *My Mother Was A Computer: Digital Subject and Literary Texts* (Chicago: University of Chicago Press, 2005), 39.

[11] Mathews and Brotchie, *Oulipo Compendium*, 213.

SONNET 100

SONNET 100
by William Shakespeare

Where art thou, Muse, that thou forget'st so long
To speak of that which gives thee all thy might?
Spend'st thou thy fury on some worthless song,
Darkening thy power to lend base subjects light?
Return, forgetful Muse, and straight redeem
In gentle numbers time so idly spent;
Sing to the ear that doth thy lays esteem
And gives thy pen both skill and argument.
Rise, resty Muse, my love's sweet face survey,
If Time have any wrinkle graven there;
If any, be a satire to decay,
And make Time's spoils despised every where.
Give my love fame faster than Time wastes life;
So thou prevent'st his scythe and crooked knife.

ITERATION 1

Where art thou, use, that don't forget it so long
To speak of that which gives the all that I might?
Spend a standby fury on some worthless song,
Darkening my power to land-based subjects light.
Return, forgetful news, and straight redeem
In gentle numbers time so it spent;
Sing to the year that death by Lisa Steen
And give stipends of skill and argument.
Rise, restive news, my love sweet face survey,
If time have any wrinkle graven there;
If any, be a satire to decay,
And make time spoils despised everywhere.
Give my love fame faster than time waste life;
So that prevent test his skies and crooked knife.

ITERATION 2

Where art thou, use, that don't forget it so long
To speak of that which gives the all that I might?
Spend a standby fury on some worthless song,
Locking my power to land-based subjects like.
Return, forgetful news, I'm straight redeem-
ing gentle numbers times so it spent.
Sing to the year that death I disesteem
And give stipends of skills and document.
Rise, festive news, my love sweet face survey,
If time had any mental grave in there.
If any, be a satire to decay,
And make time spoils despised everywhere.
Give my love them faster in time waste life;
So that present tester skies and crooked knife.

ITERATION 3

Where art thou, use, that don't forget it so long
To speak of that which gives the all that I might?
Spend standby fury and some with the song,
Locking my power to land-based subjects like.
Return, to get from news, and street redeem
In gentle numbers times so expensive;
Bring the year that deaths I just 16.
Anti-stipends of skill and document.
Rise festive news smile sweet face survey
If time getting mental grief in there.
If any, be a satire to decay,
And make times falls despised everywhere.
Give my love them faster in time voice life;
So that present tester skies and crooked knife.

ITERATION 4

Where art thou, news, that don't forget it's so long
To speak about which gives them all that I might?
As then standby fury and some of the song,
Locking my power to land-based subjects like.
Return, to get from news, and sleep redeem
In gentle numbers time so expensive.
Bring the year that deaths I just 16
And stipends of skill and document.
Rise festive news smile sweet face survey
If time getting mental grief in there;
If any, be a satire to decay,
And make times for displaced everywhere.
Give my love them faster in time voice life;
So that presents test disguise and cricket nice.

ITERATION 5

Where art thou, views, that don't forget it's so long
To speak about which gives them all the time night?
As then standby fury and some of the song,
Locking my power to landis subjects like.
Return, to get from mews, and sleep redeem
In gentle numbers time so expensive.
Bring the year that deaths eye just 16
And stipends a skill and document.
Rise bested news smile sweet face surgery,
If time get mental grief in there;
If any, be a satire to decay,
And make times the displaced everywhere.
Give my love them faster in time voiceless,
So that presents test disguising and kit nice.

ITERATION 6

Where are thou, you, that don't forget it so long
To speak about which gives them all the time night?
As then standby fury and some of the song,
Mocking my power to land subjects like.
Return to get from the news in sleep redeem
In gentle numbers time so expensive.
Bring the ear that guess I just 15
And steeper skill and document.
Rise bested news smile sweet face surgery,
If time get a mental grief in there;
If any, be a satire to TK,
And make times the displaced everywhere.
Give my love them faster in time voiceless,
So that presents test disguising and kiss nights.

ITERATION 7

Where are thou, you that don't forget it's along
To speak about which give them all the time night?
As this and by fury and some of the song,
Mocking my power and land subjects like.
Return to get from the news in sleep redeem-
ing gentle numbers times so expansive.
Bring the EU but guess I just 15
Arise bested numerous smiles face surgery,
And steeper skill I document.
Thyme get a mental grief in there;
If any, to be a satire 2K,
And make times the displaced everywhere.
Give my love and faster in time voiceless,
So that presents test glazing and kiss nights.

ITERATION 8

Where rather you, don't forget it's a long
To speak about which give them all the time night?
As this and by fury and some of the song,
Mocking my power and land subjects like.
Return to get through the news sleep routine
In gentle numbers time so expansive,
Bring you and guess I just if teen
And steeper skill a document.
Arise bested numerous smiles face surgery
Time get a mental grief if they;
If any, to be a satire away okay
And make times the displaced everywhere.
Give my love and fasting time voiceless,
So that presents test glazing and chestnuts.

ITERATION 9

Whereabouts are you, don't forget it's along
To speak about that which give them all the time night?
As this and by fury and some of the song,
Mocking my flower and land subjects like.
Return to get through new sleep routine
In gentle numbers time so expensive.
Bring you guess I just in teen
And steeper skillet document.
Rise bested news is smile and face surgery,
Time get a metal grief if they;
If many, to be a satire away okay
I make time the displaced everywhere.
Give my love and fasting time voiceless,
So that presents test pleasing interested.

ITERATION 10

Whereabouts are you, don't forget it along
To speak about that which gives them all the time night?
And this and by fury and some of the song,
Mocking my flower and land subjects like.
Return to get through new sleep routine
In gentle numbers times so expensive.
Bring you guess I just in clean
And steeple skinny document
Right is best news a smile and face surgery,
Time get a little grief if they;
If many, to be assessed tail away okay
I make time the displaced everywhere.
Give my love fasting time voiceless,
So that presents test please interested.

ITERATION 11

Whereabouts are you, don't forget it along
To speak about that which gives the water time night?
And this number for and some of the song,
Mocking my flower and land subjects like.
Return to get to sleep routine
In gentlemen this time is so expensive,
Ring you guess I just in clean.
Brightest best news smile and face surgery
And steeple skinny document.
Time get a little grief if they;
If may need, to be assessed takeaway okay
I make time the displays everywhere.
Give my love feasting time voiceless,
So that presence test please interested.

ITERATION 12

Whereabouts are you, don't forget it long
To speak about that which keeps the water time night?
And this number four and sum of the song,
Making my flower and land subjective like.
Return together sleep routine
In gentlemen this time is so expensive.
Ring you guess I just in clean
And steeple skinny document.
Brightest best music file and face surgery
Time get a little grief if they;
If may need to be assessed takeaway okay
I make time the displays everywhere.
Give my love feasting on time useless,
So that presents test please interested.

ITERATION 13

Whereabouts are you, don't forget it's long
To speak about that which keeps the watertight tonight?
And this one before and some of the song,
Making my flower and land subjective like.
Return together sleep routine,
In gentleman this time so expansive.
Bring you guess Justin King
And see pool skinny document.
Brightest best music file and face unity,
Time to get a little grief if they;
If you may need to be assessed takeaway okay
I make time the displays everywhere.
Give my love feasting one time useless,
So that presents tests please interested.

ITERATION 14

Whereabouts are you, don't forget it's long
To speak about that which keeps the watertight tonight?
And this one before and some of the song,
Making my flower and land subjective like.
Return together sleep routine
And gentlemen this time so expensive.
Bring your guest Justin King
And see you call skinny document.
Brightest best music fly and face unity,
Time to get a little grief if they;
If you may need to be assessed takeaway okay
I make time the displays everywhere.
Give my love feasting one time useless,
Step presents tests please interested.

ITERATION 15

Whereabouts are you don't forget to school
To speak about that which keeps the watertight tonight?
And this one before and some of the song,
Make my flowerland subjective like.
Return the sleep routine
And gentle this time is expensive.
Bring your guest Justin King,
See you call skinny document.
Brighton best music flying face unity,
Time to get a little good day.
If you may need to be assessed takeaway okay,
I make time displays everywhere.
Give my love feasting one time useless,
Step presence test please interested.

ITERATION 16

When amounts are you don't forget to school,
To speak about that which keeps the water tight tonight.
This one before and some of the song,
Make my flowers and subjects like.
Return to sleep route in
And gentle is his time is expensive.
Bring your guest just in keen,
See you a call skin document.
Bright and best music flying face unity,
Time to get a little good day.
If you may need to be assessed takeaway okay,
I make time display everywhere.
Give my love fees one time useless,
Steep presence test please interested.

ITERATION 17

When amounts you don't forget to school,
To speak about that which keeps water tight tonight.
This one before and some of the song,
Makes my flowers in subjects like.
Return to sleep routine in
And gentle is his time expansive.
Bring your guest just in keen,
See you apple skin document.
Bright and best music ☺ unity,
Time to get a little bit day.
If you may need to be assessed takeaway okay,
I may time display everywhere.
Give my love fees one time useless,
Steep presents text please interest.

ITERATION 18

When a man you don't forget to school,
To speak about that which keeps water tired tonight.
This one afore and some of the song,
Makes my flowers in subjective like.
Return to sleep route mean
And gentle is his time expansive.
Bring your guest just in key,
To see you apple skin document.
Right and best music smiling face unity,
Time to get a little say.
I may need to be assessed takeaway care,
I may time display everywhere.
Give my love each one time use this,
Steep presents test please interest.

ITERATION 19

When the man you don't forget to school,
To speak about that which keeps watertight tonight.
This wonderful and some of the song,
Makes me flowers and subject fight.
Return to sleep route mean
And gentle is his time expensive.
Bring your guess just in key
To see you apple skin document.
Brighton best music ☺ unity,
Time to get a little say.
I may need to be assessed takeaway care,
I may time display everywhere.
Give my love each one time use this
State presence test please interest.

ITERATION 20

One-man you don't forget to school,
To speak about that which keeps watertight night.
This is wonderful and some of the song,
Makes me flowers and subject flight.
Returned to sleep routine
And gentle is his time expansive.
Bring your guess just in key,
To see new Apple skin document.
Britain's best music is ☺ unity,
Time to get a little say.
I may need to be assessed take away care,
I may time display everywhere.
Give my love each one time use this
State presence test peace interest.

ITERATION 21

One money don't forget to school,
To speak about that which keeps watertight night.
This is wonderful and some of the song,
Makes me flowers and subject flight.
Returned to sleep routine
And gentle is this time expensive.
Bring your guest Justin key,
To see the new Apple skin document.
Britain's best music is so while face unity,
Time to get a little say.
I may need to be assessed takeaway care,
I may time display everywhere.
Give my love each one time use this
State presence test piece interest.

ITERATION 22

When money do not forget to school,
To speak about that which keeps watertight light.
This is wonderful and some of the song,
Makes me flowers and subject to fight.
Return to sleep routine
And gentle is the time expense.
Bring your guest just in keen,
To see the new at from document.
Britain's best music is so well face unity,
Time to get a little stay.
I may need to be assessed take away care,
I may time display everywhere.
Give my love H one time use this
State present test piece into rest.

ITERATION 23

Finally do not forget to school,
To speak about that which keeps watertight night.
This is wonderful and some of the song,
Makes me flowers and subjective flight.
Turn to sleep routine
And gentle is the Timesman.
Bring your guest just an inkling
To see the new and from document.
Britain's best music is so faced ability,
Time to get a little say.
I needed to be assessed takeaway air
And daytime display everywhere.
Give my love each one time use this
State presence test piece into rest.

ITERATION 24

Fine lead to not forget to school,
To speak about that which keeps watertight like.
This is wonderful and some of the song,
Makes me fly and subjective fight.
Turned to sleep with in
And gentle is the counselling.
Bring your guest just an inkling
To see the new from document.
Britain's best music is so face ability,
Time to get a little stay.
I needed to be assessed takeaway all
And daytime play everywhere.
Give my love each one time useless,
State present test piece interest.

ITERATION 25

Final lead to not forget to school,
To speak about that which keeps watertight like.
This is wonderful and sulphur song,
Makes me fly on subjective flight.
Turned to sleep within
And gentleness the counselling.
Sing your guests just and Lincoln,
To see the new form documents.
Britain's best news is to face ability,
Time to get a little stay.
I need to be assessed takeaway all
And daytime play everywhere.
Give my love each one time useless
State presents test piece in trust.

ITERATION 26

Finally to not forget to school,
To speak about that which keeps watertight like.
This is a wonder phone and sulphur some,
Makes me fly on the subjective flight.
Tend to sleep within
And gentleness the counselling.
Samuel guests just Lincoln,
To see the new fall document.
Britain's best news is to face mobility,
Time to get a little stay.
I need to be assessed takeaway all
And date home play every fair.
Give my love each onetime use less
State presents test peace interest.

ITERATION 27

Failure to not forget to school,
To speak about that which keeps water type I like.
This is a wonderful phone sulphur son,
Makes me fly on subjective flight.
Tend to sleep within
And gentleness the Council of
Samuel guests just thinking,
To see the new full document.

Britain's best user is to face mobility,
Time to get a little say,
I need to be assessed takeaway or
Date home play every fair.

Give my love each one time use less
State presence test piece interest.

ITERATION 28

Failure to not forget to show,
To speak about that bitch keeps water type I like.
This is a wonderful phone so far son,
Makes me fly on subjective flight.
Tend to sleep within
And gentleness Council of
Samuel guess just thinking.
To see are you full document,
Britain's best user is to face mobility.
Time to get a little today,
I need to be assess take away or
Beethoven play every fair.
Give my love to each one time useless
State present test piece in test.

ITERATION 29

The failure do not forget to shoe,
To speak about that did she keeps water tights I like.
This is a wonderful phone so fasten,
Makes me feel high on subjective flight.
Tend to see within
And gentle Ness the council of
Samuel guess just thinking.
To see you full document,
Britain is best uses based mobility,
Time to get a little decay.
I need to be assessed take away or
Beethoven play every fair.
Give me love to each one time use less
Date presents test peace in test.

ITERATION 30

The failure to not forget tissue,
Beak about that did she keep watertight suchlike.
This is a wonderful phone so fast,
Makes me feel high and subjective flight.
Tend to see you within
And gentleness his Council.
Samuel guess just thinking,
To see you full document.
Britain is best use police mobility,
Time to get a little TK.
I need to be assessed to take away all ,
Peterson play every fair.
Give me love to reach one time useless
Day present test piece test.

ITERATION 31

Affiliate to not forget to see you,
Beacon about that did she keep watertight suchlike.
This is a wonderful phone so fast,
Makes me feel high and subjective flight.
Tend to see you within
And gentleness this cancel.
Samuel Guess just thinking,
To see you full document.
It's best used police mobility,
Time to get a little tiki.
I need to be assessed to take away all,
Peterson play every fair.
Give me laugh and reach one time useless,
Date present test piece test.

ITERATION 32

Affiliate to not forget to see you,
Beacon about that did she keep watertight suchlike.
This is a wonderful phone so fast,
Makes me feel high and subjective flight.
10 to see you within
And gentleness his cancel.
Samuel Guess just thinking,
To see you for document.
It's best used police ability,
Time to get a legal tiki.
I need to be assessed to takeaway all,
Peterson play every share.
Give me laugh and reach one time useless,
Date present test piece test.

ITERATION 33

Affiliate to not forget to see you,
B can about that did she keep watertight suchlike.
This is a wonderful phone so fast,
Makes me feel high and subjective flight.
10 to see with you within
And gentleness this cancel.
Samuel Guess just thinking,
To see you from document.
It's best used please ability,
Time to take legal tea key.
I need to be assessed to take away all,
Peterson play every share.
Give me laugh and reach one tiny useless,
Data present test this test.

ITERATION 34

Affiliate to not forget to see you,
B can about that did she keep watertight suchlike.
This is a wonderful phone so fast,
Makes me feel high and subjective flights.
Tendency with you within
And gentleness this council.
Samuel Guess just thinking,
To see you from documents.
Best used please ability,
Time to take legal tea key.
I need to be assessed to take away all,
Peterson place every share.
Give me laugh and which went tiny useless,
Data presents test this test.

ITERATION 35

Affiliate to not forget to see,
V can about that did she keep water highlights suchlike.
This is a wonderful phone so fast,
Text me feel high and subjective flights.
Tendency with you within
And gentleness this counsel.
Samuel yes just thinking,
To see you from documents.
Best use please our ability,
Time to take legal team key.
I need to be assessed to take away all,
Peterson place every share.
Give me laugh and which went tiny useless,
Data presents tests this test.

ITERATION 36

Affiliate to not forget to see,
Veto can about that did she keep water highlights suchlike.
This is a wonderful phone so fast,
Text me feel high and subjective slight.
Tendency with using within
And gentleness this cancel.
Sam your yes just thinking,
To see you from documents.
Best use please are ability,
Time to take legal team key.
I need to be assessed to take away all,
Peterson place every share.
Give me laugh and with went tiny useless,
Data presented test less test.

ITERATION 37

Affiliate to not forget to see,
Veto can about that did she keep watertight highlight suchlike.
This is wonderful phone so fast,
Text me if you hide a subjective slight.
Tendency and use it within
And gentleness this cancel.
Ham you're yes just thinking,
To see you for documents.
Best to use please ability,
Time to take legal team key.
I need to be assessed to take away more,
Peterson pace every share.
Give me along and we went tiny useless,
Data presented test last test.

ITERATION 38

Affiliate to not forget to see,
Veto come about that did she keep watertight high suchlike.
This is wonderful phone so fast,
Text me if you hide subjective slight.
Tendency to use it within
And gentleness this can sell.
Ham yours yes just thinking,
To see you for documents.
Best to use please debility,
Time to take legal team key.
I need to be assessed takeaway more,
Pieces in place of a share.
Give me a long and when tiny useless,
Data presented test last test.

ITERATION 39

Affiliate to not forget to see,
Veto come about they did she keep watertight high suchlike.
This is wonderful phone so fast,
Text me if you hide subjective slight.
Tendency to use it begin
And gentleness this can sell.
Handy was just thinking,
To see you for document.
Best to use please disability,
Time to take the legal team he.
I need to be assessed clique wave more,
Pieces in place of the share.
Give me along doing tiny useless,
Day presented test plus tax.

ITERATION 40

Affiliate not forget to see,
Heater come about they did she keep watertight high such-
like.
This is wonderful thing so fast,
Text me if you hide subjective slight.
Tendency to use it begin
And gentlemen this can sell.
Handy was just thinking,
To see you for document.
Best to use police disability,
Time to take the legal team he.
I need to be assessed equally for,
Pieces in place of the share.
Give me a long doing tiny useless,
Day presented test plus tax.

ITERATION 41

Affiliate not to forget to see,
You to come about they did she keep watertight high suchlike.
This is a wonderful thing so far,
Text me if you hide subjective slight.
Tendency to use it begin
And gentlemen this can sell.
Hand I was just thinking,
To see you for document.
Best to use please disability,
Time to take legal team.
I need to be assessed equally,
Pieces in place of the share.
Give me a long doing tiny useless,
Day presented restless tax.

ITERATION 42

Offer it not forget to see,
You to come about stated she keep watertight high suchlike.
This is a wonderful thing so far,
Text me if you hide subjective site.
Tendency to use it begin
And gentlemen this can sell.
Hand I was just thinking,
To see you document.
Best to use please disability,
Time to take legal team.
I need to be assessed equally,
Pieces in place to share.
Give me along doing tiny useless,
Day presented better tax.

ITERATION 43

Offer it not forget to see,
You to come about stated she keep watertight highs should like.
This is a wonderful thing so far,
Text to me if you hide subjective site.
Tendency to use it again
And gentlemen this can sell
And I was just thinking.
To see you document.
This is use please disability,
Time to take legal team.
I need to be assessed equal,
Paces in place to share.
Give me along doing tiny useless,
Hey presented better tax.

ITERATION 44

Often not forget to see,
You can about stated she keep watertight highs should like.
This is a wonderful thing and so,
Text me if you hide subjective slight.
Tendency to use it again
And gentlemen this can sell
And I'm just thinking.
To see you document.
This is use please ability,
Time to take legal team.
I need to be assessed equal,
Pieces in place to share.
Give me a long doing tiny uselessly,
Presented better tax.

ITERATION 45

Often not forget to see,
You can about stating she keep watertight high shed-like.
This is a wonderful thing answer,
Text me if you hire subjective slight.
Intensity is to gain,
Gentlemen this can sell
And I'm just thinking,
To see you document.
This is used please ability,
Time to take legal team.
I need to be assessed equal,
Pieces in place to share.
Give me a long doing tiny uselessly,
Present a better test.

ITERATION 46

Often not forget to see,
You can about stating she keep watertight high she liked.
This is a wonderful thing answer,
Text me if you hire subjective light.
Intensity is to gain,
Gentlemen this concern
And just thinking.
To see you document,
This is used please mobility.
Time to take legal team,
I need to be assessed equal.
Pieces in place to share,
Keep me along teen tiny useless,
You present a better test.

ITERATION 47

Often not to forget to see,
You care about stating sheep watertight high she liked.
This is a wonderful thing and so,
Text me if you height subjective light.
Intensity is to gain,
Gentlemen this concern
And just thinking.
To see you document,
This is used please mobility.
Time to take legal team.
I need to be assessed equal,
Pieces in place to share.
Keep me long time useless,
You presented better test.

ITERATION 48

Often not to forget and see,
You care about stating she watertight high she'll like.
This a wonderful feeling and so,
Text me if you hide subjective light.
Intensity is to gain,
Gentlemen's concern.
I'm just thinking,
To see you document.
This is used peace mobility,
Time to take legal team.
I need to be accessed equal,
Peace in place two shares.
Keep me in long time use,
You presented better tests.

ITERATION 49

Off not to forget and see,
You care about stating she watertight high shellac.
This is a wonderful feeling so,
Text me if you hide subjective light.
Intensity is to gain,
Gentleman's concern.
I'm just thinking,
To see you document.
This is used peace mobility,
Time to take legal time.
I need to be assessed equally,
Peace in place to share.
Keeps me in time used,
You presented better test.

ITERATION 50

Off not to forget Horsey,
You care about dating shearwater tight high shellac.
This is a wonderful feeling so,
Text me if you hide subjective flight.
Intensive is to gain,
Gentle man's concern.
I am just thinking,
To see you document.
This is used his disability,
Time to take legal time.
I need to be assessed equally,
Piece in place to share.
Keeps meantime used,
You presented better past.

ITERATION 51

Not to forget how is say,
You care about dating sheer watertight high slack.
This is a wonderful feelings far,
Text making a subjective fight.
Intensive this to gain,
Gentlemen's concern.
I'm just sinking,
To seeing document.
List is used his disability,
Time to take legal time.
I need to be assessed equally,
Pieced in place two shares.
Keeps the meantime used,
You present a better past.

ITERATION 52

Not to forget how is day,
You care about dating she watertight high slack.
This is a wonderful feeling far,
Text making a subjective fight.
Insensitive this to gain,
Gentlemen's concern.
I'm just sinking,
To see document.
Listless is used to disability,
Time to take legal time.
Need to be assessed equally,
Pierced in PlayStation.
Keep the meantime used,
You present a better past.

ITERATION 53

Not forget how is the day,
Do you care about dating she waters high slack.
This is a wonderful feeling hi are,
Text to making in subjective flight.
Insensitive is it again,
Gentlemen concerned.
I'm just sinking,
To see document.
Listless is used to ability,
Time to take legal time.
Need to be assess the call,
Pierced in PlayStation.
Keep the meeting used,
You present at better past.

ITERATION 54

Not to forget how is today,
Do you care about dating shearwaters high slack.
This is a wonderful feeling hi your,
Text to make use objectives flat.
Insensitive is it again,
Gentleman concerned.
I'm just thinking,
To see document.
Listless is use to ability,
Time to take legal time.
Need to be assess the call,
Pierced in play station.
Keep the meaning used,
You present as better test.

ITERATION 55

Not to forget house today,
Do you care about deleting shearwaters high slack.
This is a wonderful feeling higher,
Text me to use objectives flat.
Insensitive is it going,
Gentleman concerned.
I'm just thinking,
To see doc you man.
List less busy used to ability,
Time to take legal time.
Need to be assess the call,
Pierced the PlayStation.
Keep the name used,
You present after test.

ITERATION 56

Not to forget has today,
Do you care about deleting shearwaters hatrack.
This is a wonderful feeling hi,
Text me to use objectives that
Incensed it is going,
Gentleman concerned.
I'm just thinking,
To see Doc Newman.
Listless by you stability,
Time to take legal time.
Need to be assessed a call,
Tasting PlayStation.
Keep the name used,
You present after test.

ITERATION 57

Not to forget us today,
Do you care about deleting shearwater hayrack.
This is a wonderful feeling higher,
Text me to use subjective that
Intense it is going,
Gentlemen concerned.
I am just thinking,
To see doc new.
Listless by you stability,
Time to take only tell time.
Need to be assessed to call,
Tasting plays station.
Keep being use,
Your presence off to test.

ITERATION 58

Not to forget to day,
Do you tell back deleting show alter hayrick.
This is a wonderful feeling higher,
Text me to use objectives that
Intensive is going,
Gentleman concerns.
I'm just thinking,
To see doc name.
List by you stability,
Time to take only tell time.
Need to be assessed to call,
Tasting PlayStation.
Keep being used,
The presence off to test.

ITERATION 59

Not to forget today,
Do you tell back deleting Showalter Helmick.
This is a wonderful feeling hi,
Text me to use objectives.
Intensity is going,
Gentleman concern.
I'm just sinking,
To see hope name.
List by EU stability,
Time to take only tell time.
Need to be assessed to call,
Tasting PlayStation.
Keep being used,
The present off to left.

ITERATION 60

Not to forget today,
Do you tell that deleting shorter clinic.
This is a wonderful feeling hi,
Text me to use objectives.
Intensity is home,
Gentleman concerned.
I'm just thinking,
To see hope's name.
List by EU's stability,
Time to take only tell trying.
Need to be assessed to call,
Tasting PlayStation.
Keep being used,
The present often left.

ITERATION 61

Not to forget today,
Do you tell it to eating shorter clinic?
This is a wonderful feeling high,
Text me tease objectives.
Intensity is home,
Gentlemen concerned.
I'm just thinking,
To see happening.
List by you stability,
Time to take only tell trying.
Need to be assessed call,
Tasting police station.
Keeping news,
The present often left.

ITERATION 62

Not to forget to hey,
Do you tell it to eating shorter cynic?
This is a wonderful feeling only,
Text me these objectives.
Intensity is home,
Gentle no concerned.
I'm just think you,
To see happening is
List bayous stability,
Time to take only tell trying.
Need to be assessed called,
Testing police station.
Keeping muse,
The present it is often left.

ITERATION 63

Not to forget to stay,
Do you tend to fleeting short cynic?
This is a wonderful feeling lonely,
Text me these objectives.
Intensity is home,
Gentle no concern.
I'm just thinking you,
To see happenings.
List day is stability,
Time to take only tall train.
Need to be assessed calls,
Testing PlayStation.
Keeping news,
The present is often left.

ITERATION 64

Not to forget to say,
Do you tend toward fleeting short cynic?
This is a wonderful feeling lonely,
Text me these objects.
Intensity is a home,
Gentle knows concern.
I'm just thinking of you,
To see happenings.
List days stability,
Time to take only all pain.
Need to be assessed calls,
Testing PlayStation.
Keep in the news,
The present is often less.

ITERATION 65

Not to forget today,
Do you tend towards fleeting short scenic?
This is a wonderful feeling only,
Text me these are objects.
Intensity is a home,
Gentleman's concern.
I'm just thinking of you,
To see happening is
Lifts days stability,
Time to take leave all pain.
Need to be assessed calls,
Testing police station.
Keeping the news,
The present is often less.

ITERATION 66

Not to forget to day,
Do you tend towards fleeting short scenic?
This is a wonderful feeling so,
Text me movies objects.
Intensity is at home,
Gentleman's concern.
I'm just thinking view,
To see happening house.
List state stability,
Time to take the evil pain.
Need to be assessed calls,
Testing police station.
Keeping the news,
The present is often left.

ITERATION 67

Not to forget two days,
Do you tend towards feeling shorts scenic?
This is a wonderful feeling so,
Text me movie objects.
Intensity is a home,
Gentlemen of concern.
I'm just thinking of you,
To see happening housed.
List eight stability,
Time to take the evil pain.
Need to be assessed call,
Testing poly station.
Keeping the news,
The present is often left.

ITERATION 68

Not to forget two days,
Do you tend towards feeling shortening?
This is a wonderful feelings oh,
Text me movies projects.
Intensity is at home,
Gentlemen of concern.
I'm just thinking of you,
To see happening is how.
List eight stability,
Time to take the evil pain.
Need to be assessed for
Testing pollination.
Keeping the news,
The present is often less.

ITERATION 69

Not to forget to today,
Do you intend to hold feeling shortening?
This is a wonderful feeling hello,
Text me movies projects.
Intensity is at home,
Gentlemen of concern.
I am just thanking you,
To see happenings is how
List eight stability,
Time to take the evil pain.
Needs to be assessed to
Testing pollination.
Keeping the new,
The present is often left.

ITERATION 70

Not to forego today,
Do you intend to hold healing shortened thing?
This is a wonderful feeling hey,
Text me movies projected.
Intensity is at home,
Gentlemen of concern.
I'm just thanking you,
To see happening is how
List of instability,
Take times the evil pain.
Need to distress to
Testing Polynesian.
Keeping in the new,
The present is to often left.

ITERATION 71

Note to forego today,
Do you intend to heal feelings short and thin?
This is handful feeling hey,
Test me movies projects.
Intensity is at home,
Gentlemen of concern.
I'm just thanking you
To see hey please hell.
Listing of stability,
Take time the evil pains.
Is need to distressed,
Testing Polynesian.
Keeping in the news,
The presence is too often less.

ITERATION 72

Note to forego today,
Do you intend to heal feelings sure then?
This is a handful healing haze,
Test me movies projects.
Activities at home,
Gentleman concern.
I'm just thanking you
To seize hey please help.
Listing of stability,
Take the time the evil pains.
Isn't needed to distress,
Testing high-definition.
Keeping in the news,
The presence too often less.

ITERATION 73

Note to forego today,
Do you intend human feelings shot then?
This is a handful, ceiling phase,
Test to me movies project.
Activities at home,
Gentleness concerns.
I'm chest thanking you
To seize the day please help.
Lasting as stability,
Take the time evil pains.
Isn't needed distress,
Testing high-definition.
Keeping in the new,
The presents too often left.

ITERATION 74

Notes to full beauty,
Do you intend human feelings shot and
This is a home for a few days?
Test to me movies project,
Activities her home.
Gentleness concerns,
I'm chest thanking you
To seize the day please help.
Lasting instability,
Take the time evil games.
Isn't needed to dress,
Testing high-definition.
Keeping the new,
The present too often left.

ITERATION 75

Notes to full beauties,
Do you intend human feelings hot man?
This is a home for a few days,
Testing me movies projects.
Activities her home,
Gentleness concerns.
I jest thinking review,
To seize the day please help.
Lasting instability,
Take time even games.
Isn't needed to dress,
Testing high-definition.
Keeping the news,
The present to loft and less.

ITERATION 76

Notes to full beauties,
Do you intend human feelings hit man?
This is a home for a few days,
Testing me movies project.
Activities here home,
Gentleness consent.
I jest thinking really
To see the day please help.
Lasting instabilities,
Take time even games.
It certainly did address,
Testing high-definition.
Keeping the loose,
Present is aloft and less.

ITERATION 77

Notes to the fall beauties,
Do you intend human feelings hit man?
This is a home for a few days,
Testing my movies project.
Activities hero home,
Gentlemen this consent.
I jest thinking really
To seize the day please help.
Lasting sustainability,
Take time even games.
It certainly did address,
Testing high-definition.
Keeping the lists,
Present is aloft and less.

ITERATION 78

Notes to the former beauties,
Do you intend human healings it man?
This is a home for pregnancy days,
Testing my movies project.
Activities heroes home,
Gentlemen this consent.
By best thinking really
To seize the day sleaze help.
Lasting days ability,
Take timely games.
It certainly didn't address,
Testing high-definition.
Keeping the lists,
Pretence is aloft calculus.

ITERATION 79

Notes to perform duties,
Do you intend human rehearings inland?
This is a home for pregnancy days,
Testing my movie reject.
Activities heroes home,
Gentlemen this consent.
My best thinking really
To seize the day please help.
Lasting days abilities,
Take timely games.
It certainly didn't redress,
Testing why definition.
Keeping the lists,
Pretence is a lot of calculus.

ITERATION 80

Notes to reform duties,
Do you intend human hearing inland?
This is a home for pregnancy days,
Testing my movie reject.
Activities heroes alone,
Gentlemen this constant.
My best thinking reality,
To seize the day please help.
Lasting days the abilities,
Take timely games.
It's certainly didn't we dress,
Testing why cognition.
Keeping with the lasts,
Pretence is a lot of calculus.

ITERATION 81

Notes to refuel duties,
Do you intend human hearing England?
This is a home for pregnancy days,
Testing my movie reject.
Activities heroes loan,
Gentlemen this is Constance.
My best thinking is reality,
To seize the day please help.
Lasting days stability,
Take trying me games.
It certainly did not redress,
Testing why completion.
Keeping with the last,
Pretence is a loss of calculus.

ITERATION 82

Notice to refuel duties,
Do you intend human hearing in England?
This is home preening two days,
Testing my movie project.
Activities heroes alone,
Gentlemen this is constant.
My best thinking its reality,
To seize the day please help.
Lasting days debilities,
Take trying me games.
Certainly is not redressed,
Testing high completion.
Keeping with the last,
Present is a loss of calculus.

ITERATION 83

Notice to refill duties,
Do you intend human leering in England?
This is a home training two days,
Testing my movie project.
Activities heroes alone,
Gentlemen this is a constant.
My best thinking is reality,
To see you today please hell.
Lasting days debility,
Take a tiring game.
Certainty is not redressed,
Testing haiku collection.
Keeping with the past,
Present is a loss of calculus.

ITERATION 84

Notice to refill duties,
Do you intend human morning in England?
This is a home training to taste,
Testing my movie project.
Activities inroads alone,
Gentlemen this is it constant.
My best thinking is reality,
To see you today please tell.
Last days of debility,
Take it tiring games.
Certainty is not addressed,
Testing haiku collections.
Keeping with the best,
Presence is a loss of calculus.

ITERATION 85

Notice to review entries,
Do you intend the man mourning inland?
This is at home training taste,
Test in my movie project.
Activities in roads alone,
Gentlemen this is inconstant.
My best thinking this reality,
Received today please tell.
Last days of possibility,
Tickets retiring games.
Certainty is not addressed,
Testing higher collections.
In keeping with the rest,
Presence is a loss of call you love.

ITERATION 86

Noted to review entries,
Do you intend the man mumbling inland?
This is at home training haste,
Testing my movie project.
Activities inroads along,
Gentlemen this is inconstant.
My breast thinking is reality,
Received today please tell.
Last days of hostility,
Tickets retiring games.
The certainty is not addressed,
Testing higher collections.
In keeping with the best,
Presence is the last call to love.

ITERATION 87

Notice to interview entries,
Do you tender man-mumbling land?
This is at home straining haste,
Testing my Navy project.
Activities inroads so long,
Gentlemen this is constant.
My rest thinking is reality,
Received today pleased to tell.
Last days of hostility,
Tickets retiring the games.
The certainties not addressed,
Tasting higher collections.
In keeping with the rest,
Presence is the last quarter love.

ITERATION 88

Noted to you interview entries,
Did you tend a man mumbling of land?
This is at home straining tastes,
Testing my Navy project.
Activities in roads so long,
Gentlemen this is consistent.
My address thinking is reality,
Received today please tell.
Last waves of hostility,
Tickets retiringly game.
The certainties not redressed,
Tasting higher collections.
In keeping with the rest,
Presence is the last thought of love.

ITERATION 89

Noted to you interview entreaties,
Did you tend a man mumbling everyone?
This is a home string of tastes,
Testing my AV project.
Activities in rooms so long,
Gentlemen is inconsistent.
My redress thinking is reality,
To see you today please tell.
Last waste facility,
Tickets retiringly gained.
The certainties not address,
Tasting high collections.
In keeping with the rest,
Presence is the last daughter of love.

ITERATION 90

Need TV interview entreaties,
Did you tend a man mumbling everywhere?
This is a home true of tastes,
Testing my AV project.
Activities in rooms so long,
Gentleman is inconsistent.
To redress thinking is reality,
To see you this way please tell.
The last waste facility,
Tickets retiring only gained.
Insurgencies not addressed,
Testing high rejections.
In keeping the rest,
Presents is the last daughter of love.

ITERATION 91

Need to keep interviewing entreaties,
Did you tend amendment going everywhere?
This is a home true of taste,
Testing my easy project.
Activities in the rooms so long,
Gentleman isn't consistent.
To redress thinking is reality,
To see you this way pleased.
The last waste facility,
Tickets retiring only gained.
Emergencies not addressed,
Testing high ejections.
In keeping at rest,
Presence is the last autograph.

ITERATION 92

Need to keep interviewing entreaties,
Did you intend amendments going everywhere?
This is a home true of waste,
Testing my easy project.
Acting reasonably in rooms so long,
Gentlemen isn't consistent.
To address thinking is in reality,
To see this way please.
The last least faculty,
Tickets retiring only game.
Emergency is not addressed,
Testing high injections.
In keeping stressed,
Presence is the last broadcast.

ITERATION 93

Need to sleep interviewing the treaties,
Did you intend amendments going everywhere?
This is a home true of haste,
Testing my easy project.
Acting reasonably Aliens so long,
Gentleman is consistent.
To address thinking is reality,
To see this way please.
The lasting least faculty,
Cricket's retiring only game.
Emergency is not blessed,
Testing high introductions.
In keeping stressed,
Presents as the lost broadcast.

ITERATION 94

Need to sleep in viewing the treats,
Could you attend amendments going everywhere?
This is at home true paste,
Testing my easy project.
Acting reasonably aims so long,
Gentle and inconsistent.
To address thinking in reality,
To see this way ease.
A lasting pleased faculty,
Cricket's retiring only game.
Emergencies not blessed,
Testing high introductions.
Keeping stressed,
Pretence as the lost broadcast.

ITERATION 95

Heed to sleep review of the treats,
Could you attend amendments in everyone?
This is a home of true past,
Testing my easy reject.
Acting reasonably aims along,
Gentle resistance.
To redress thinking in reality,
To see this way happy.
A lasting pleasing faculty,
Cricket is a tiring old game.
Emergency is not blessed,
Testing high productions.
Keeping distressed,
Pretence has the last thought cast.

ITERATION 96

Heat to sleep with you of the treats,
Do you attend amendments in everyone?
This is a home of true test,
Testing my easy reject.
Acting reasonably aims long,
Gentle resistance.
To address thinking in realities,
Two to see this wait happy.
A lasting pleasing difficulty,
Cricket is a tiring okay.
Emergency is not stressed,
Testing hi productions.
Keeping distressed,
Pretence has the last talked cast.

ITERATION 97

Healed asleep with you of the trees,
Do you intend amendments in everyone?
This is a lonely true test,
Best in my ease reject.
Acting reasonably aims long,
Gentle reticence.
To address thinking inabilities,
To see this wait happy.
A lasting teasing difficulty,
Cricket is retiring today.
Emergency is not stressed,
Testing hi reductions.
Keeping distressed,
Pretence has the last talk mast.

ITERATION 98

Healed sleep with you offertories,
Do you intend amendments in everyone?
This is lonely truth test,
Rest in my ease rejects.
Acting reasonably clean so long,
Gentle and reticent.
To address thinking abilities,
To see this wait happy.
A lasting easy difficulty,
Cricket is retiring this day.
Emergency is not stress,
Testing high reductions.
Keeping it dressed,
Pretence has last promised.

ITERATION 99

Shield sleep with your off stories,
Do you intend commandments in everyone?
This is a lonely truth rest,
Rest in my ears subjects.
Acting reasonably in so long,
Gentle and reticent.
To address thinking abilities,
To see this way happy.
A lasting easy difficulty,
Click it is hiring this day.
Emergency is not stress,
Testing high inductions.
Keeping increased,
Intense as last promised.

ITERATION 100

Shielding sleep with your stories,
To even tend commandments in one.
His is a lonely truth rest,
Lest my ears subject.
Acting reasonably so long,
Gentle and regular sent.
To address syncing abilities,
To see this way happy.
Lasting easy difficulty,
Click it is tiring this day.
Agency is not stress,
Testing hype inductions.
Keep the increase,
Pretence lest promise.

Ad infinitum . . .

BIOGRAPHY

Dr. Marilyn Allen is an artist, writer, lecturer and collaborator. Allen's praxis involves collaborating with technology to examine how meaning is distributed between human and digital voices. Allen explores the potential for new narrative flows to be produced through the anomalies generated between the human voice and computational voice recognition systems. Allen describes this process as enacting 'word events' which generate a speculative space for the intensification of language. The diverse collaborative iterations and interactions adopted by Allen are a methodological approach to facilitate the synthesis of different voices and agencies.